The Wretched Stone

CHRIS VAN ALLSBURG

Houghton Mifflin Company   Boston   1991

To W.L.

Library of Congress Cataloging-in-Publication Data
Van Allsburg, Chris.
    The wretched stone / Chris Van Allsburg.
        p. cm.
    Summary: A strange glowing stone picked up on
a sea voyage captivates a ship's crew and has a terrible
transforming effect on them.
    ISBN 0-395-53307-4
    [1. Sea stories.] I. Title.
PZ7.V266Ws   1991   91-11525
[Fic]—dc20   CIP
                             AC

Printed in the United States of America
HOR 10 9 8 7 6 5 4 3 2 1

The type is set in Garamond #3 by Monotype Composition.
The paper is Paloma Matte, supplied by Consolidated Papers.
Both text and jacket are printed by Acme Printing Company.
The books are bound by Horowitz/Rae.

EXCERPTS FROM THE LOG

of the

Rita Anne

RANDALL ETHAN HOPE,

CAPTAIN

May 8

We finished bringing supplies aboard early this morning. At midday we left on the tide and found a fresh breeze just outside the harbor. It is a good omen that our voyage has begun with fair winds and a clear sky.

May 9

The first mate, Mr. Howard, has brought together a fine crew. These men are not only good sailors, they are accomplished in other ways.

Many read and have borrowed books from my small library. Some play musical instruments, and there are a few good storytellers among them.

May 17

Our passage is going well. The usual boredom that comes with many days at sea is not present on this ship. When the members of this clever crew are not on duty, I find them singing and dancing or amusing each other with tales of past adventure.

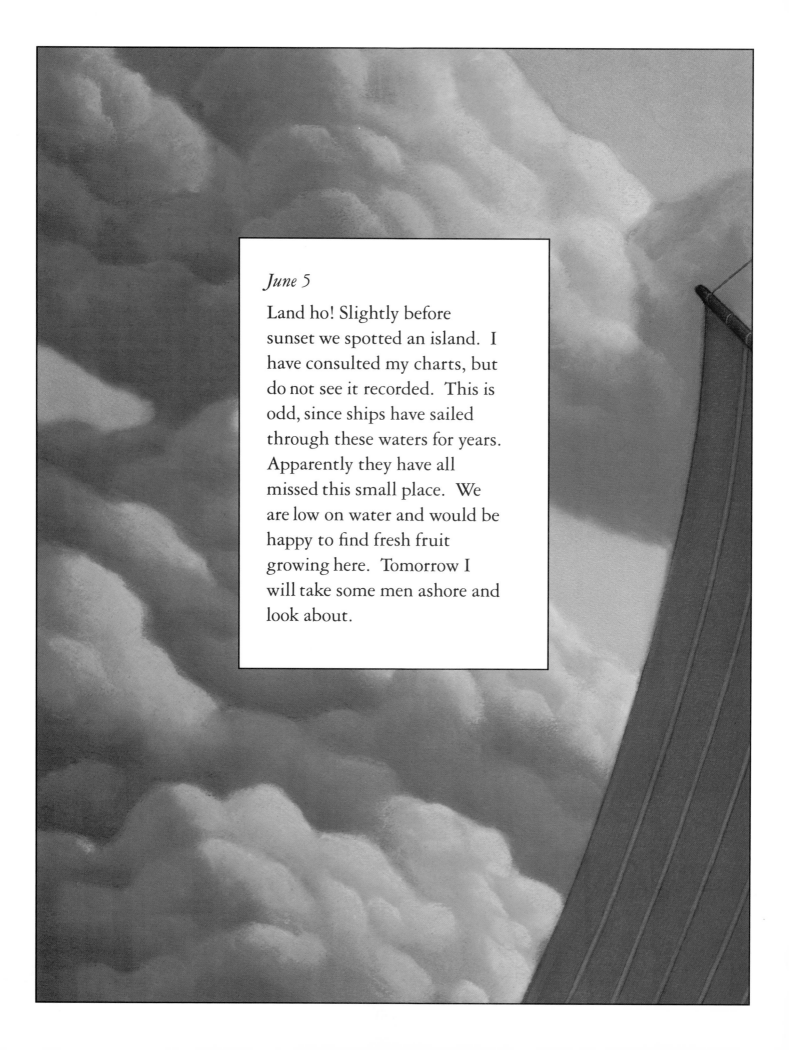

June 5

Land ho! Slightly before sunset we spotted an island. I have consulted my charts, but do not see it recorded. This is odd, since ships have sailed through these waters for years. Apparently they have all missed this small place. We are low on water and would be happy to find fresh fruit growing here. Tomorrow I will take some men ashore and look about.

June 6

I have just returned from the
island. It is strange indeed. The
vegetation is lush, but not a
single plant bears fruit. The air
has an odor that at first seems
sweet and pleasant, then
becomes an overpowering stink.
I saw no sign of animal life, not
even an insect. We found a
spring that had water too bitter
to drink. We also discovered
something quite extraordinary,
which I have brought aboard.

It is a rock, approximately two feet across. It is roughly textured, gray in color, but a portion of it is as flat and smooth as glass. From this surface comes a glowing light that is quite beautiful and pleasing to look at. The thing is unbelievably heavy, requiring six strong men to lift it. With great effort we were able to get it aboard and into the forward hold. We have set sail and are under way again.

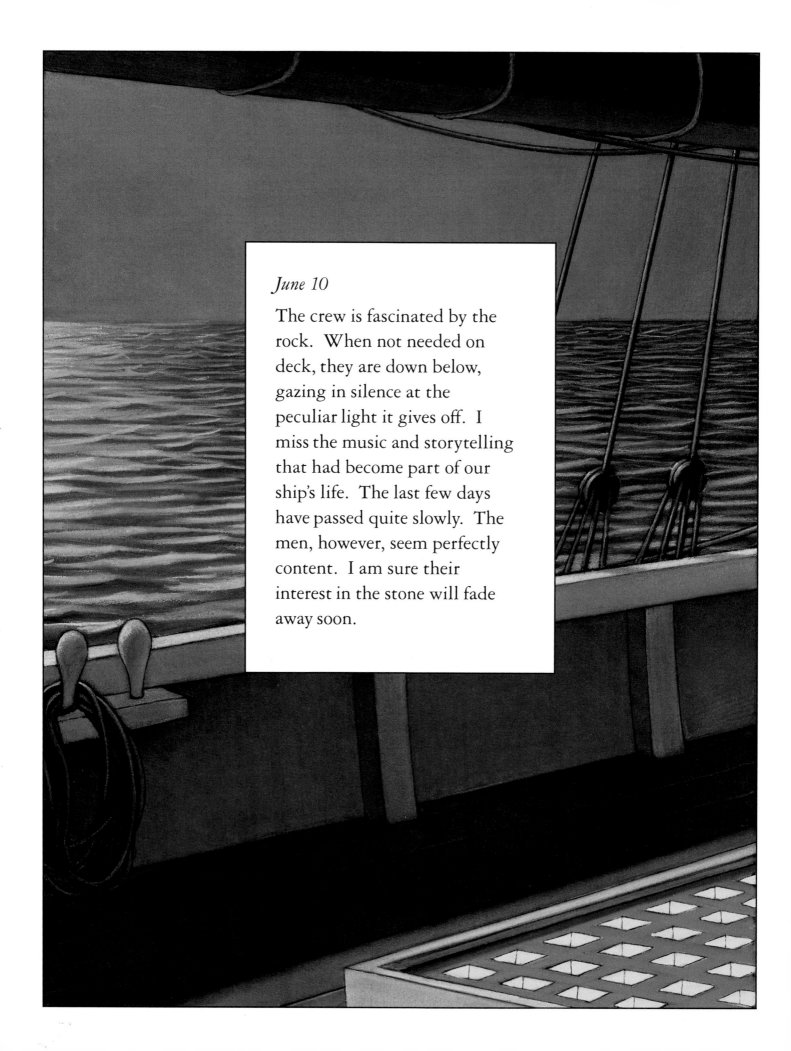

June 10

The crew is fascinated by the rock. When not needed on deck, they are down below, gazing in silence at the peculiar light it gives off. I miss the music and storytelling that had become part of our ship's life. The last few days have passed quite slowly. The men, however, seem perfectly content. I am sure their interest in the stone will fade away soon.

June 13

Something is wrong with the crew. They rarely speak, and though they swing through the rigging more quickly than ever, they walk the decks in a clumsy, stooped-over fashion. Last night I heard shrieks coming from the forward hold. I believe they have contracted some kind of fever that came on board with the stone. I told Mr. Howard that tomorrow I will have the thing thrown overboard.

June 14

This morning I awoke to find the deck deserted. The wheel was tied steady with a rope. I believe Mr. Howard, who spent some time around the rock, told the men about my plan to get rid of it. They have now locked themselves in the forward hold. They apparently believe, in their feverish state, that I can sail this boat alone while they sit around that wretched stone.

June 15

We are in grave danger. A powerful storm is headed this way. All morning long the wind has grown steadily stronger; the sky is filled with dark clouds. I am unable to shorten the sails by myself. With this much canvas up, we will surely be blown over and sink when the full force of the storm arrives. I am going forward again to try to get the crew to work. All our lives depend on it.

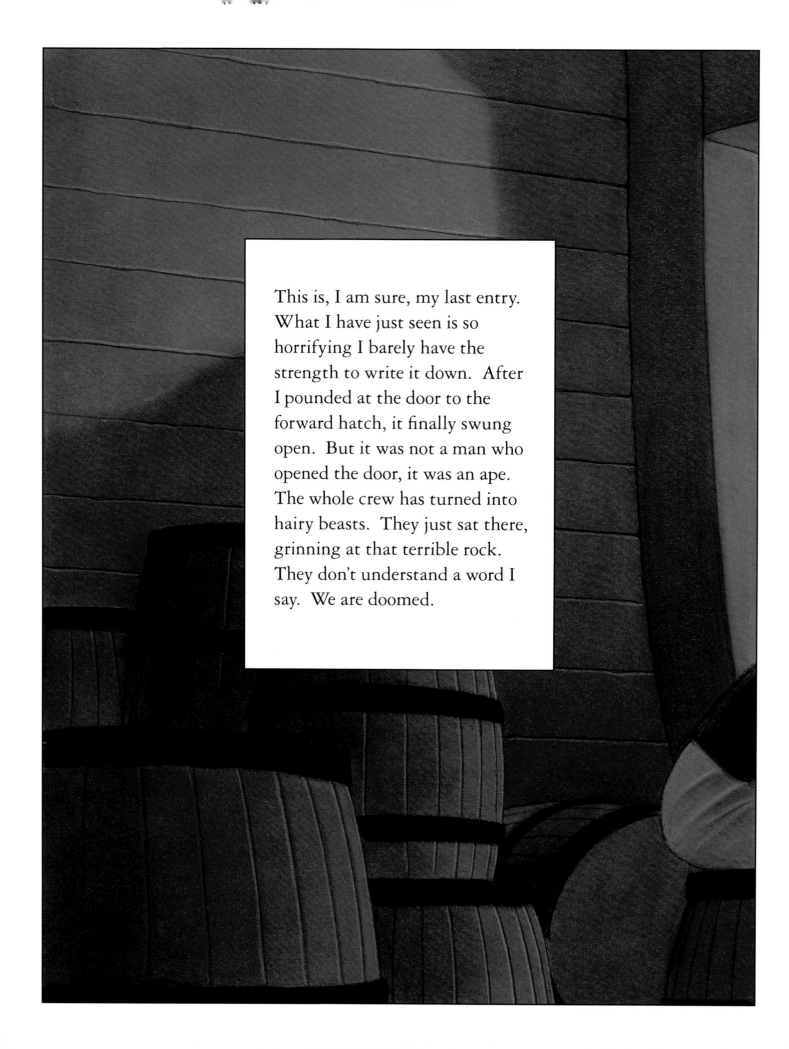

This is, I am sure, my last entry. What I have just seen is so horrifying I barely have the strength to write it down. After I pounded at the door to the forward hatch, it finally swung open. But it was not a man who opened the door, it was an ape. The whole crew has turned into hairy beasts. They just sat there, grinning at that terrible rock. They don't understand a word I say. We are doomed.

June 16

The storm has passed. The *Rita Anne* is still afloat, but both masts and rudder are lost. The stone has gone dark. We were struck by lightning twice during the storm. I believe that was the cause. Unfortunately, the crew is unchanged. They are still beasts, but seem sad and lost without the glowing rock. I have moved them back to their quarters. We have food for two weeks. I am hopeful of a rescue.

June 19

I have made an encouraging discovery. I am playing the violin and reading to the crew. It is having a positive effect. They are walking upright and have an alert look in their eyes.

June 24

I was in the forward hold today. A dull glow was coming from the stone. I have covered it and will keep the compartment locked.

June 28

I am happy to report that the men have returned to normal. It seems that those who knew how to read recovered most quickly.

June 30

We are saved! A ship has been spotted off our starboard side. I have decided to scuttle the *Rita Anne*. There is only one place for the wretched stone. Before we abandon ship, I will set a fire that will send this vessel and her cargo to the bottom of the sea.

July 12

Our rescuers have left us in the
harbor town of Santa Pango.
One by one the crew should be
able to sign on to ships passing
through and work their way
home. We have made an
agreement not to talk about the
strange events that took place
aboard the *Rita Anne.* The
men appear to have recovered
completely, though some
show an unnatural appetite for
the fruit that is available here.